Y0-ABZ-759

CHILDREN LEARN PHYSICAL SKILLS

Vol. 1
birth to 3 years

Liselott Diem

CHILDREN LEARN PHYSICAL SKILLS

Vol. 1
birth to 3 years

Liselott Diem

Published in the United States of America by the American Alliance for Health, Physical Education and Recreation, Washington, D.C., in agreement with the copyright holder, Kosel-Verlag GmbH & Co., Munich, West Germany.

Originally published under the title, *Kinder Lernen Sport.*
© 1974 by Kosel-Verlag GmbH & Co., Munich

English translation by the American Alliance for Health, Physical Education and Recreation, with the able assistance of Mrs. Barbara Buve, Berlin, West Germany and Dr. Reinhard Bergel who also served as consultant. Dr. Helen M. Eckert of the University of California, Berkeley, reviewed the manuscript, as did the author, Mrs. Liselott Diem, Koln, West Germany.

FOREWORD

The American Alliance for Health, Physical Education and Recreation is privileged to present a translation of Liselott Diem's *Kinder Lernen Sport* Birth to Age Three. In Germany, the word *Sport* means more than athletic skills and games so we have translated the title to *Children Learn Physical Skills*. The author, from Germany, is a world recognized leader, interpreter and designer of physical education programs for children. For years she has been in great demand as a lecturer, demonstration teacher and inspirational speaker concerning the physical growth and development of children and appropriate activities to enhance that development.

Today in the United States there is a rapidly growing interest and concern for appropriate environment and educational programs for the very young child with special concern for infant care and development. Certainly, physical development needs appropriate attention. Thus, it is timely for AAHPER, as a national educational organization concerned with the health and well-being of individuals, to translate her book. The presentation of this work does not necessarily include the endorsement of the methodological approach of the author which at times appears somewhat didactic and antithetical to the philosophy of many of the early childhood leaders in the United States.

Nevertheless it is a valued work and worthy of use for ideas, inspiration and discussion by persons concerned about infant development in the United States.

AAHPER presents this as part of an international contribution to the literature in the field surrounding the growth and development of infants and children and also has translated her book on *Kinder Lernen Sport* Ages 4-6.

Margie R. Hanson
Elementary Education Consultant
American Alliance for Health,
Physical Education and Recreation

CONTENTS

Preface

Introduction

SECTION 1: FIRST DIRECTED IMPULSES

1. The Newborn Child Is Used to Motion   2. The Prone Position Stimulates the Child's Getting Up   3. Skin Contact Practices the Sense of Movement   4. Associated Movement   5. Ability to Push Up and Support the Body   6. Walking, Climbing, and Swimming Abilities   7. Gripping and Clasping Ability   8. Flexible Fingers and Sure-Grip Hands   9. Flexible Toes and Supportive Feet   10. The Child Stands Up Alone

SECTION 2: THE SENSE OF PERCEPTION BECOMES REFINED

11. Differentiated Feeling, Pressing, Crumpling and Grasping   12. Space Orientation in a Jumper Seat   13. Following the Rolling Ball   14. Sounds and Rhythms   15. A Variety of Situations   16. Solving Problems Independently

SECTION 3: PLAYING WITH A PARTNER

17. Hanging and Flying   18. Rocking in a Hoop   19. Learning the Proper Use of Strength   20. Showing Resistance   21. Playing "Horsey"   22. Increasing the Difficulty of the Activities   23. Balancing Freely and Jumping Off   24. Piggy Back with Variations   25. Holding the Suspended Position   26. Posture   27. Climbing Up and Turning Over   28. Handstand   29. Trying Out His Own Strength on an Object

SECTION 4: ORIENTATION TO SURROUNDINGS

30. Climbing Safely Up and Down   31. Up and Down with Hands and Feet   32. Jumping Off (Dismounting)   33. Crawling Through   34. Swinging Back and Forth Independently   35. Swinging Back and Forth While Hanging from a Bar   36. Somersaulting and Rolling   37. Sureness of Space Orientation through Ball Playing   38. Kickball Games

SECTION 5: LEARNING TO USE ONE'S SKILLS

39. Open Space and Fast Running   40. Ability to Adjust While Running   41. Jumping High   42. Jumping Over Obstacles   43. Broad Jumping   44. Creating New Exercises   45. Creativity   46. Recognition of One's Own Possibilities and Limitations   47. Moving Slowly in a Concentrated Manner   48. Types of Sports that Train the Balance   49. Accuracy of Movement   50. The Child Needs to Learn in a Group

PREFACE

Already the first days and weeks of life are decisive for the development of the child's movement abilities. Recognizing this fact, Volume 3 in the series *Kinder Lernen Sport* (*Children Learn Physical Skills*) tries to give parents, teachers and educators ideas for the promotion of motor development during the first three years. (*Editor's Note*: Volume 3 in the original German series has been made Volume 1 in the English translation and Volume 4 is Volume 2.)

In 50 chapters, aids are given for a sensible and systematic advancement of the infant and small child. In this an entire area of movement is omitted: swimming for the small child. Two other volumes in the series concentrate on this — *Swimming in the First and Second Years* and *Swimming in the Third and Fourth Years*. The learning program of the entire series is set forth in two additional volumes with didactical sport suggestions and introduction for children up to ten years old.

Kinder Lernen Sport is not to be thought of as a training for the performance of the child, but indicates how the child learns through objective stimulations to maintain and expand movement abilities in limited surroundings.

Good health also depends on mastered activities in running and climbing; whoever experiences satisfaction and success in skills moves more and increases movement intensity. The book offers aids to the individual forms of movement of the child, which should not be based on the standards of the adults, but should help the child in his own way of life. Do not conform to a certain system, but become a partner for your child in the movement activities.

Liselott Diem
Cologne, March 1974

INTRODUCTION

For the child, movement is a fundamental aid in getting to know his own environment. In order to use it fully, he needs different motivations in the first years of life. Volume 3 of the five part series *Kinder Lernen Sport* (*Children Learn Physical Skills*) gives examples for the development of the movement skills and the ways in which the child prepares himself for activity. From being moved to moving oneself — between these two extremes lies the far reaching scale of the learning processes for the first two years.

The child's ability for movement at birth must be continuously expanded. In Volume 1 of the series we showed as an example in the swimming of the infant, how intelligently a child already reacts to suitable contact aids during the first weeks of life. Here the examples are further expanded.

In part, these new forms of play demand a readjustment by the parents and educators who have contact with the infant and small child. With the aid of movement experiences they develop curiosity, a feeling of well-being and later interest and insight. Parents feel themselves to be partners with the small child. To be a partner in this sense means not only to give the child stimulating ideas, but also to let oneself be stimulated through the child. The early experiences with a partner are especially important for the social behavior of the child.

Self-movement is a basic self-experience for the child. When he moves along, he notices new spaces, relationships, and problems and challenges. Movement learning goes beyond the comprehending of movement processes; it is at the same time producing emotional and cognitive experiences, i.e. those beneficial to the understanding. Through his movement ability, the child develops his perceptive, creative, coordination abilities and also with this his sense of balance, space, and time. He gains insights and develops through this his intelligence, logical behavior and self control. The understanding and recognizing of the individual abilities and limitations become clear. In the second and third year, play areas and toys should above all be varied to give the child the opportunities to be imaginative and creative. The independent application of what has been learned is the goal of movement training.

Learning sports does not mean producing sport achievements, but rather behavioral ability and movement intelligence in association with others and in new situations. It also means appropriately mastering the technical difficulties of a challenge with pleasure.

Every learning demands daily practice. In the first weeks of life, there should be five periods daily of 5 to 10 minutes each available for this before eating; up to six months, three periods daily of 30 minutes each for movement activities. Later the child needs at least three periods daily, 1 to 1½ hours, in which he can independently pursue his movement interests with toys, self invented situations, stimulated through a partner or a group to expand his abilities.

The male pronoun is used in this book and for convenience was not changed in the translation; the pronoun is intended to apply equally to both sexes.

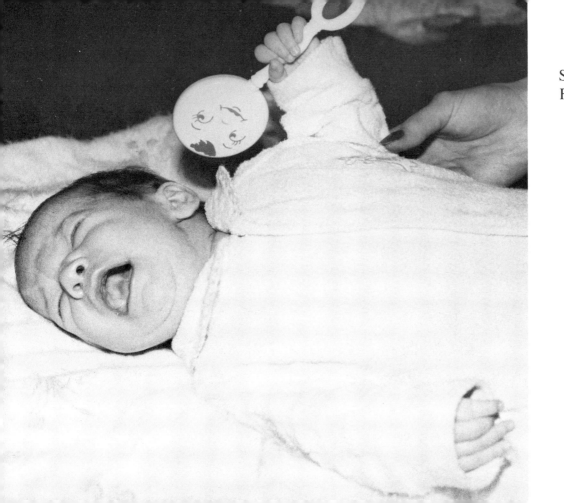

SECTION 1.
FIRST DIRECTED IMPULSES

1. The Newborn Child Is Used to Motion

Some nations count the day of birth already as the first birthday. They demonstrate with this the unity of the prenatal development period with the time thereafter. It becomes clear how close the connection is as one observes a newborn child. Immediately after the birth, the child can already:

- lift his head
- push himself up with his toes from the prone position
- kick his legs
- go forward with crossed legs and use his toes and feet actively on the floor when held up
- try to climb up when held against one's body
- grasp with his fingers as his hands are touched, grasp with the toes as the sole of the foot is touched.

The newborn is capable of doing these things because he has already gained astonishing movement abilities in the first months of the prenatal phase! He bends and stretches his legs and moves his toes, fingers, and hands in many different ways. He turns his head and sucks his thumb. Beyond this the unborn child can already recognize sounds and light intensities.

Therefore, the newborn is neither insensitive nor inactive. However, he is dependent on our assistance. His self-initiative depends on the manner in which we help him to develop his movement, (motor) sensory, speech, and thinking abilities. No doubt, the newborn already needs our directed stimulation.

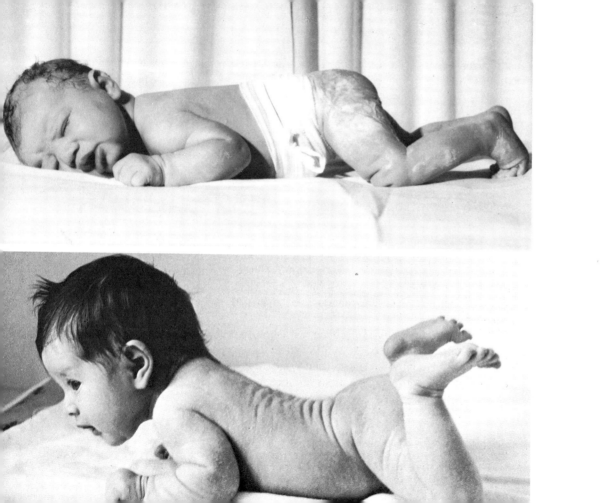

2. The Prone Position Stimulates the Child's Getting Up

For the learning of movement, the position of the child plays a special role. The child should lie mainly on the stomach, since in this position he can learn to help himself.

- He practices the sensitive feeling of the hands and feet, of the fingers and toes through touching, feeling, clasping, grasping and pushing.
- He learns to raise his head through the strength of his back muscles.
- He realizes his success as he lifts himself up and sees more of his surroundings.
- He breathes deeper and more quietly.

The newborn should also change position to lie on his back and on his sides; in the first few days he needs stimulants for changing his position. In the time when he is awake, carry and hold him in different ways. Through his experience in the time before birth, the child is used to changing from a vertical to a horizontal position. The newborn above all needs freedom of movement:

- no tight baby diapers, but diaper pants, as little clothing as possible according to the temperature
- no hard or soft mattress, but a firm elastic one which absorbs movement and supports the body.

3. Skin Contact Practices the Sense of Movement

The infant's awareness increases through the way in which he is touched, held and picked up. Therefore, our skin contacts are very important as a signal system for his sensation of movement. The sense of movement is sensitized by the pressing and touching receptors of the skin.

Moreover, the warm skin contact supports the feeling of security and continues the close union in which the child lived before birth.

- Use every opportunity to lay the infant on your bare skin.
- Press him close to you in different positions, horizontally or vertically. Cradle him slowly and quietly back and forth. This gives the infant a feeling of security and pleasure.
- Be careful that you do not touch the child with very cold hands.

Not only the skin but also the water belongs to the touch impulses of the infant. The kinaesthesia (perceiving of his own movements) is strengthened if the child can move freely with his whole body while bathing. Unfortunately most baby bathtubs are too small, or the child is held in the wrong way so that he cannot move freely back and forth. The water temperature for an infant should not be more than 88°F. The movement impulses slacken if the water is too warm.

4. Associated Movement

The child practices his movement and sensory abilities by the way in which we touch him with our hands, i.e. how we turn him around, lay him down, or dress and undress him. Mothers as well as fathers must first learn this necessary awareness to support the sensitivity of the child in different ways and measures. The infant learns to move by adjusting himself to the movement of the adult. When he is carried he feels every movement of the adult. Unconsciously and passively he practices to orient himself in a room and to differentiate between movements. Investigations have shown that children who were carried around a lot had a higher level of development and advanced motor certainty.

The mother and father should also:

- carry the child around as much as possible
- carry the child in different ways and manners (vertically, horizontally, on the hip, on the back, and later on the shoulders)
- when carrying the child, change the rhythm, tempo and direction of the pace. The child should feel the change in the movement. Observe at the same time his signs of satisfaction, i.e. by a quiet turning or by an up and down motion.
- repeat motions to which the child reacts happily and let him gradually consciously play along
- avoid hastiness, violence, and all too sudden changes. Through these, the child becomes afraid.

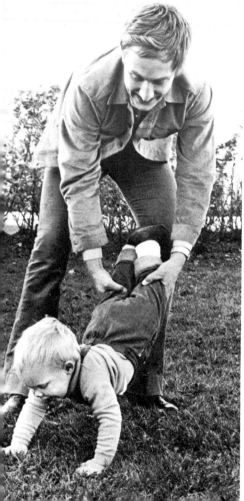

5. Ability to Push Up and Support the Body

The newborn reacts with his reflexes through resistance. When you put his feet on the floor, he pushes himself up stiffly. Placing the feet firmly against the floor is the first step for the child to stand up. Through different exercises, you can systematically motivate a nine-week-old child to increase his attempts. He does possess the necessary strength to do this. Through the practiced kicking of the legs during the prenatal period, he has strong leg and foot muscles.

- Hold the child so that he can place his feet on the floor.
- Encourage him to spring up and down while you always gently support his movements.
- Encourage him to push up and support his body weight with his feet more consciously and strongly.
- When you do these exercises using different foundations (mattress, table), the child will learn to differentiate in his reactions.
- For a change the child can, while you sit on a chair, try to push himself up while you move your thighs up and down.

As with the legs, the child also supports himself reflexively with his arms and hands when you hold him head down to the floor. You can also encourage him in this support (stem) position to spring up and down. Shoulders, arms, hands and fingers react elastically and gradually the child looks for the stem position and these up and down motions. Already at the age of four months, the child can do knee push ups alone or while standing move up and down holding on to the bed or chair.

6. Walking, Climbing and Swimming Abilities

The newborn moves his legs in a turned-in forward-crossed fashion. This can appear in different forms as if the child were trying to make walking, swimming, or climbing movements — the feet and toes are especially active. Every individual toe grasps and pushes itself away. This flexibility must be maintained. Therefore avoid:

- tight wrapping of the feet, socks or shoes; the foot covering serves only as warmth and protection and must be as soft and wide as possible.
- overweight; it impedes the mobility of the child. Infants are often overfed.

Encourage the child to stand up or climb in various situations. In the bathtub, there should also be the opportunity for stretching movements of the legs and feet. Since the child needs room for this, take him from the second month on into the big bathtub with yourself more often.

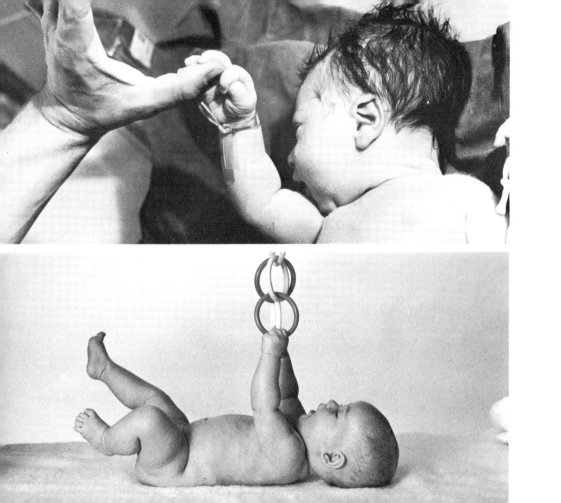

7. Gripping and Clasping Ability

Newborns possess such a strong clasping reflex that they can support their whole body with their hands while hanging. As soon as the palms of the hands are touched, the fingers grip firmly. This reflexive gripping gradually leads to conscious grasping and releasing.

You may accustom the child to different types of gripping movements and finger dexterity, if you consciously practice gripping and releasing.

- For example, hang up colored plastic or wooden rings in front of the child at which he can grab.
- Tempt the child with a swinging ring or stick to hold on to and pull himself up carefully on it for several inches.
- Use a stick or your finger, in order to stimulate the child to grab, hold, release.
- Try to develop a mutual activity through very calm stimulations and reactions.

Attempts have shown that children already at four months grasp a cup with certainty and bring it to their mouths, if they have developed their grasping ability. This activity is based on experiences which the child has had and which must again and again be offered in changing situations.

8. Flexible Fingers and Sure-Grip Hands

''This little pig went to market (thumb)
This little pig stayed home (pointer)
This little pig ate roast beef (middle)
This little pig had none (ring)
This little pig ran crying wee, wee, wee, all the way home.'' (baby)

Well-known nursery rhymes like this one play a great role when one wants to motivate the child to the differentiated finger exercises after the gripping and releasing activities. Even if the child cannot understand the words yet, he receives stimuli for his own hand and finger motions through the touching of the individual fingers, through feeling, through pushing, and through clapping. Try to give the child touch sensations by using toys made out of different materials and in different shapes.

- Rub the child's palms.
- Clap his hands gently together.
- Place objects in such a way near the child so that he can grasp and touch them.

The older the child gets, the more one should encourage the versatility of finger and hand dexterity. The older child should:

- handle a spoon and fork properly
- place glasses on the table without clanking
- learn to hang on bars, climb, and roll, catch, and throw different types of balls.

Do not forget to praise the child.

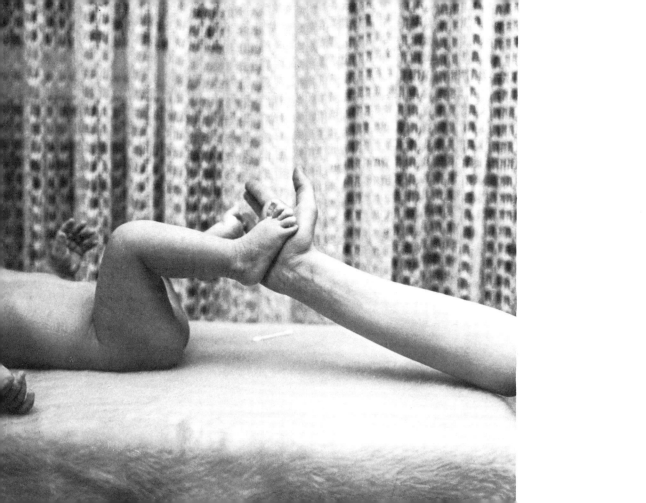

9. Flexible Toes and Supportive Feet

When a child stands up independently, he has to be able to carry and balance his own weight. His leg strength and toe flexibility, therefore, have to be further strengthened through flexibility exercises. Weakness of the feet in children can be traced back to muscle weakness and this in turn to the lack of exercise. Such a weakness can be avoided through intensive exercise of the toe muscles, since the arch of the foot is supported mainly through these little toe muscles.

The following activities strengthen the muscular structure of the foot and improve the sense of touch in the feet:

- Rub criss-cross over the soles of the feet and watch the reaction of the child, i.e. clasping of the toes.
- Push with the palm of your hand against the soles of the feet and cause a resistance through springy motions. This can lead to a regular game.
- Move the child's feet up and down, inward and outward. Always observe his reactions; the child should gradually begin to do these motions alone.
- The child likes to suck on his toes; lift his feet until his hands can touch the toes; from this, many games can result.
- Rub down and massage the child's feet and legs, from the toes to the thighs.

Above all, pay attention to the various unrestrained toe and foot movements during the first months. Avoid tight shoes. Let the child exercise with bare feet again and again.

10. The Child Stands Up Alone

Children stand up when they are able to carry their own weight. We do not put the child in the standing position, but we help him little by little to stand up by himself. In connection with this, the transitions play a big role: prone position, crawling, pulling up to an upright position, standing without support. The first free step is a difficult balance test, which requires many attempts. The child "runs" before he walks. He falls from one step into the other. The first steps are awkward and with straddled legs. A flowing walk must be practiced for a long time since it demands a sureness of body control and a refined coordination in the transition of completing a motion or movement.

- Let the child walk to you or between the mother and father. Increase the distance gradually.
- The child should walk as much as possible on different surfaces. This will help him differentiate his sense of balance and learning to walk will become easier. He can catch a cold only by standing inactively on a cold floor.

The child sometimes disrupts his walking with crawling — let him do this — this is a healthy change.

SECTION 2: THE SENSE OF PERCEPTION BECOMES REFINED

11. Differentiated Feeling, Pressing, Crumpling and Grasping

In the first years of life coordination is the most important of all sensory-motor abilities; sureness of movement is based on this. Coordination includes specifically:

- sense of balance
- ability to react
- adaptability to the situation.

Coordination ability is generally also described as dexterity. We recognize the dexterity of the child in the way in which he behaves in a new situation and how he deals with new objects. Not only does the grip and clasp sureness play a certain role, but also different perceptions open up a widened sphere of movements for the child; he learns to associate with a variety of materials; he discovers new qualities of movements through pushing, pulling, touching, seizing, releasing, crumbling.

Begin already in the first months of life to practice *these different ways* of coordination by using different types of play objects, such as:

- soft cloth, plush animals, velvet, silk, linen
- graspable pieces of wood, wooden balls, wooden sticks
- rubber animals, rubber rings.

These play objects must not only be graspable, but also colorfast, hygienic, unbreakable, and nonswallowable. Choose the colors and forms carefully. The child will soon discover a favorite toy. Give him time to play with it.

12. Space Orientation in a Jumper Seat

Already in the fifth and sixth months the child in a jumper seat learns how he can orient himself independently.

The best way is to fasten the jumper seat on a door frame or in the garden to a tree branch. The child should sit in it in such a way that he can push off with his feet and tips of his toes from the floor or ground. He will have fun bouncing up and down, turning himself, or making little jumps. Out of curiosity he will discover how he can move himself and how he can move in different directions.

- Lay a mat on the floor if it is slippery; otherwise the child won't find any resistance when pushing himself off.

The jumper seat should not be used as a "baby sitter," but should always be used to encourage a sense of play for a short time and only as long as the child moves by himself in it.

13. Following the Rolling Ball

Small children react to everything that moves: objects which swing back and forth, jump up and down, roll or fly. They also let themselves be motivated to spontaneous movement through moving objects. Thus, they like to crawl after a rolling ball — by doing this they get to know the room where they are, and also, through hanging exercises, learn to orient themselves.

- Roll the ball and crawl after it together with the child.
- By crawling the child follows the rolling ball which he sets into motion.
- Roll the ball in different directions, sometimes close to the child, sometimes farther away.

The more the child learns to follow a motion in different directions and to recognize different speeds, the more agile he will become. Unconsciously he learns to react early and in the right manner and to put his self-motion into practice.

The playing reaches its climax when the child directs the ball independently and can control it accordingly.

14. Sounds and Rhythms

The child stands in the bed holding on to the rail and moving up and down. These up and down motions make him especially happy when he can produce noises such as the mattress squeaking or the bed creaking. The reason for this amusement is the noise which is produced through these rhythmical movements.

- Take the child's hands; move them with yours rhythmically up and down or clap the child's hands rhythmically together.
- Accentuate the rhythm of the up and down or back and forth movement with the tone of your voice.
- Talk or sing to the child, even if he cannot understand the words yet.
- Encourage your child to "la, la, la," hum along or talk.
- Use rattles made of various materials or glasses which give different sounds.
- Motivate the child also through musical instruments or percussion or simply play dance music. At the same time pay attention to his reactions.
- However, show him also that hitting on different materials (wood, glass, metal) makes a different sound.
- When the child is about two years old, give him a game which is a combination of clanging toys, for example, a xylophone.

Do not get angry if the child makes noise once in a while, hits on a saucepan with a spoon, or hits the building blocks together. Through this, children discover sound and rhythm.

15. A Variety of Situations

Children need repetition, but also change. The more different the stimuli and situations are which they learn, the more they will learn to differentiate. Through experimenting the child gains new experiences and learns how to use them further. There are enough objects in the home which the child can use for his movement experiences during the first two years.

- He can learn to climb up and down on a hassock, a chair or a ladder.
- He can push chairs together and use them as a tunnel or a bridge.
- He can roll around on the rug with the aid of a pillow.
- He can use a railing to climb and hang from.

Your child will become more independent and inventive, if you:

- leave him time to experience new situations
- give him the opportunity to repeat and modify the things he has already tried once.

Only in this way will the child learn what he can handle and what his limits are. Both are equally important. Do not forbid the child to climb on anything which you are afraid he will fall down from. Rather show him how he can climb without anything happening to him. Motor learning is at the same time a cognitive and emotional process, which the child needs for his self-experience and self-assurance.

16. Solving Problems Independently

Play situations should not only be varied, but should always be presenting new problems which the child can solve. One to two-year-olds develop a direct eagerness to solve difficult tasks, if at all possible. Why? The child in doing this makes an essential discovery. He discovers that, he himself, without the help of others, has found something new and can manage it. Give your child a combination gymnastic apparatus, which you can change now and then with the aid of additional pieces. Sometimes it is a hindrance, at other times a climbing ladder, a balancing bar or a slide. The child can use his imagination on such a combination apparatus and realize it. A once discovered feat is repeated long enough until the child can handle it and it no longer appears to be a problem and becomes uninteresting.

- Develop your own problems and be patient during the problem-solving period. It is not a concern that the child should learn individual skills quickly. It matters more that the child should be able to appraise a situation independently, to recognize the problems involved, and to gain assuredness in his behavioral decisions.
- At the same time, remember that it should be fun for the child. You should not force the child nor demand too much.

SECTION 3: PLAYING WITH A PARTNER

17. Hanging and Flying

Why do children like to hang on bars so much? The hanging convinces them that they are able to support their own body weight. They are proud to be able to accomplish this. It becomes more difficult when one not only hangs still but also swings back and forth. The child is used to this rocking sensation from infancy on. Already as infants the children are rocked back and forth on the arm. From being rocked to rocking oneself is a short learning process.

- Hold the child around the torso and swing him carefully high and low. Increase the swing gradually and let him fly loosely.
- Fold your hands and let the child sit on them. Swing him between the straddled legs up and down. Now the child learns to *hold* himself and to increase the swing gradually.
- Hold the child on the thighs and swing him upside down between your straddled legs or in front of your closed legs back and forth. Children like to hang upside down like bats.
- Swing the child for a short time only, alternating with raising him up. Also, decrease the swing and let the child, hanging upside down, push himself off from the ground with his hands. Invent other games yourself.

18. Rocking in a Hoop

Every child from the first year on likes to hang on the grownup's hands and let himself be swung back and forth. From the second year on, with the use of a sturdy wooden or plastic hoop, you can elaborate on this play:

- The child sits in the hoop.
- The child stands in the hoop.
- At first the child is supported by the adult.
- The child holds on independently.

Begin carefully and let the child first be confident and show his approval. The child must go along with the movement spontaneously and should find pleasure in this. Encourage his attempts to support the swing of the hoop through body assertion and, like on a real swing, to increase the swing back and forth, up and down.

19. Learning the Proper Use of Strength

Adults can just about judge what they can lift, carry, or push and what they cannot. A child must first learn this. During play with a partner, he can best practice how much strength he should use, when the adult regulates the resistance accordingly.

- First, the child stands in a hoop, which you hold; the child leans his body against the rim and tries with all his strength to pull the adult away.
- Take a hoop, a broomstick, a piece of rope, or a scarf and try a type of tug-of-war with the child. Change these pulling games by decreasing or increasing on the pull, in order to help the child to react to different situations.
- Place an object on the floor, such as a baseball bat or a cooking pot, with both partners holding the object. Together, they push or pull the object against each other.

In these games the child is an equal partner. The assertion of strength of the adult should be equal to that of a good teacher, always just strong enough so that the child can react with the same amount of strength. Only once in a while, does the one or the other have the advantage. The child learns to react differently through the changing of the dynamic attempt.

20. Showing Resistance

Children often invent partner games in which they clasp themselves on, push away, or hang themselves with all their weight on an adult or another child. Do not look at this as a bad habit. These are important learning situations for the child since he is discovering and learning through this his own body weight. Not only the child, but also you as well, can invent such resistance games.

- Both of you lie on your backs, put your feet (soles) against each other's and try to push and kick against the resistance.
- Lift the child up, when he suddenly has hung himself around your neck as you were bending down (but only if you can!).
- Let yourself be pushed away, and at the same time, try to resist the pushing so that the child can barely master your weight.
- Try the above also in reverse and push the resisting child forward. With this also, the adult must always use only so much strength or resistance which the child can control with effort.

The success and fun in the game develop only if the result is achieved with effort and not so easily.

21. Playing "Horsey"

The whole point of the age-old child's play "horsey" lies in the dynamic change between the fast and slow tempos (from the symbolic quiet gait of the horse to the quick gallop) and in an improvised "falling down."

It depends on the age of the child, if one lets him ride on the knee or on the back. If he rides on the back, then you must observe the following:

- The child should learn how to get on and off independently. In order that he can do that, kneel down during the "getting on" stage.
- Check if the child is sitting securely and can hold on himself.
- At first go slowly forward and then gradually increase the tempo.
- Always vary the tempo and the rhythm of your movements, but always adjust them to the ability of the child. Move your backbone up and down during the "horsey" play and thereby strengthen the self-assurance of the child.
- Practice the falling off regularly, in which you slowly bend to the side. Perhaps you may wish to use a soft pillow while doing this. Create in this play certain rules, which the child understands and which he follows with pleasure.

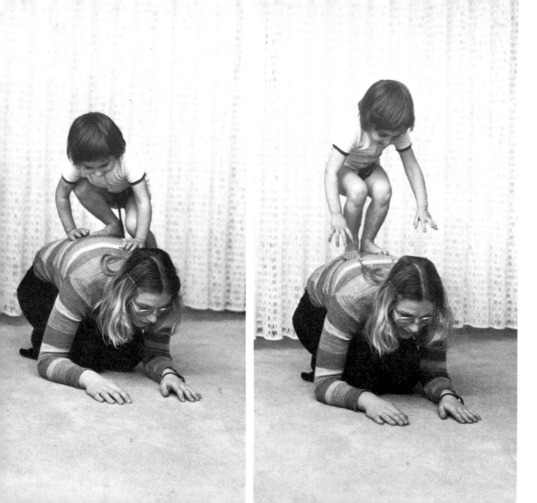

22. Increasing the Difficulty of the Activities

A one and a half year old child is no longer satisfied with the simple "horsey-play." He will have more fun if he kneels or stands on the adult's back. In this case, the adventure is more interesting, since the support area is narrower and the danger of falling off out of this height is greater.

- Prepare the child for the eventual falling down from the kneeling or standing position. From this the child should learn to roll off skillfully. A pillow also helps when practicing the "falling down."
- As soon as he feels secure in his position, crawl forward or backward, in a circle or from side to side.
- Here the point of the play lies also in the rhythm change. Through the changing reaction of the partner, the test becomes more interesting: one teases the other, for example, through the sudden movements.

This game is only attractive for the child if it is adjusted to his ability. After some vain efforts, allow the child to experience success; it must become clear to him and you: "You can shake as much as you want, I am still going to get on."

23. Balancing Freely and Jumping Off

The same topic as before is involved in balancing and jumping off. Here the precise adjustment of the child to a difficult process of movement is shown.

- The child balances freely on the back of the crouched partner.
- He pushes off firmly with the whole foot and stretches himself with loose joints during the jump.

In such a way, he keeps his equilibrium. The follow-through on the movement already shows the controlled landing possibility during the jump. This child feels secure. He can control himself and the situation.

Activities like this demand a fine degree of coordination, which only develops through repeated practice in a variety of situations. By this the child acquires situative skill and preciseness of movement abilities which will be developed only through the practicing of numerous movement processes, but not through formally written down, systematic activities.

The course of action must be found independently by the child. Only in such a way does he learn to orient himself appropriately and to react correspondingly. He learns to avoid accidents and, therefore, is not afraid of difficult situations which he is confronted with daily.

24. Piggy Back with Variations

The games of the equestrians demonstrate how skillfully the rider can juggle on his horse, how he clings, and how he adjusts himself to the galloping movements of the animal. In a similar way, we can with piggy back vary the forms of our riding games with the child:

- The child clasps himself in different ways on you and holds tight on the hips or on the back.
- You carry the child on your back. Support him first with your hands under the seat during the fast motions, until he can hold himself.
- You carry the child on your shoulders, first holding him with your hands; later he sits alone.

With these activities, it again depends on the variation of the rhythmic movement and the changing of direction. The child should learn to react and also to challenge the reactions independently. The better he learns to adjust correctly to an unexpected movement, the more self-satisfaction he feels, and his fun at this activity grows.

25. Holding the Suspended Position

The suspension hold is an important test for the stretching and balancing abilities of the child. When you hold your child around the torso and lift him up, he can stretch alone within at least four months. The child lifts the head, looks at you, and stretches the legs.

This basic form, the sense for body harmony, stretching and holding himself independently, can be varied by you in the first two years:

- Move the child up and down with springy motions while holding him with both hands over you. Increase the upward motion and release your grip shortly. The child will fly several inches into the air and will happily cry, if you do this little "air lift" carefully (see also chapter 17).
- The child supports himself with his hands on your shoulders, while you lift him by the thighs above your head. You turn around yourself or move back and forth while doing this.
- Lie on your back, pull your legs up to your chest, and have the foot soles facing up. The child lies on your foot soles and you, while bending and stretching your legs, lift him up and down holding him with both hands. Later the child can hold himself without your supporting him.

Every partner activity has an attraction through the mutual stimulating and reacting. The stimulation should also be started by the child. Do not forget: fathers and mothers are good partners, but so are also other adults or older brothers or sisters.

26. Posture

The so-called ''good posture'' is shown in the upright position and in the person's changing movement reactions. Good posture requires an upright position from the feet through the pelvis and to the shoulders. Not only does standing on the toes belong to this upright position, but also the free hanging, which children like to try especially on the horizontal bar.

- Let your child hang from your hands or from bars or rings, if they are available.
- Encourage him while hanging to rock back and forth and to increase the swing.
- When the child hangs on your hands, change your own posture. For example, lift or lower the arms or change the direction of the swing without the child giving up the hanging position.

Contrary to this, the child must tighten his buttock muscles and hold and stretch himself, when lifted in the following way:

- Hold the child on the thighs and lift him up. This strengthens the pelvic position and the body unity, which he has already practiced through the suspension position.

By the way the child gets himself into the swinging motion, you can tell about his posture. If he lacks strength, he will hang with slumped shoulders; he does not lift his head free of the shoulders. If a child has weak muscles, start with easy exercises in which he does not need to carry his whole weight.

27. Climbing Up and Turning Over

If your child has often been able to support and pull his own body weight and has developed sufficient trunk strength, the following activities will be easy:

- Hold the child by both hands. Get him to climb up on your thighs so high that with his head down, and his legs up, he can turn headover and end up standing.
- When the child has mastered this exercise, you can increase the difficulty: He can go back the same way, i.e. lift his weight up out of the hanging position and swing back. When your child can do this, he has strength in his torso.
- Vary the exercise through the use of a pole (broomstick) which you hold with both hands, over which the child can swing up and turn around.
- It becomes more difficult when you take two rubber rings in the hands and try the same experiment with them.

When you do not have a horizontal bar, you should try as much as possible to increase the activities of the climbing up and turning over with your child. In this way you make your child independent and establish prerequisites for posture.

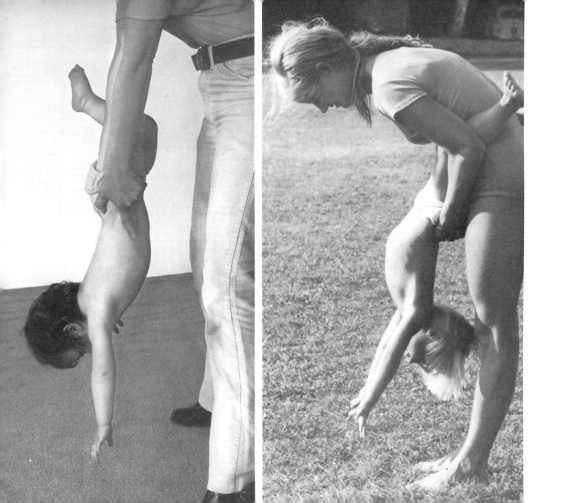

28. Handstand

Already in the first weeks of life, you were able to observe the so-called "jump reaction." As soon as the child hangs with his head down, he instinctively supports himself with his arms and hands in order to catch his body weight. We made use of this reaction in order to let the few-months-old child try out the supporting strength of his arms (see also chapter 5). You can increase these exercises:

- Hold the child on the thighs with the head down until he can touch the floor with his hands. Lift him up and down in a springy motion until he takes the initiative to push off himself.

The child sits on the hip of the adult and lets himself glide down backwards until he can touch the floor with his hands. When he feels secure, you can release his legs from your hips so that he can turn over onto his feet.

Repeat the handstand in an altered situation, for example:

- Let the child climb up the wall with his feet while he supports himself with the hands.

Children love games where they stand on the head or hold the head down in order to see the world "upside down."

29. Trying Out His Own Strength on an Object

Pulling, pushing, lifting, carrying belong to the analyzing of objects in the environment which tempt the child to try out something. He pushes the child's stroller, he tries to carry a child's chair, or the three-year-old tries to carry a smaller child. Children need these strength tests:

- By this they learn their pushing ability or the thrust of their body.
- They vividly experience their success; the object which they have chosen can be moved.
- They learn cooperation, since they often pull each other or help each other to push a heavy object.

The exercises should not be too simple and the objects not too light. An easily reached goal is not much fun. As in every game, the demands must be appropriate to the child's ability. The child must, even if at first with concentrated effort, be successful.

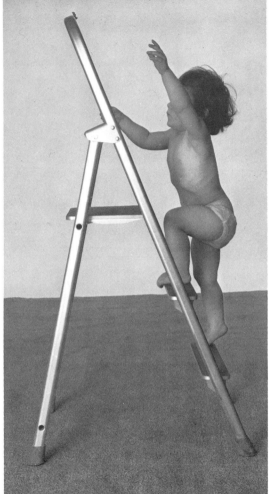

SECTION 4: ORIENTATION TO SURROUNDINGS

30. Climbing Safely Up and Down

Space orientation is gained by the child only through active games. Opposites such as up-down, high-low, behind-in front, left-right must be learned independently and on his own before the child can distinguish between them. He must learn, for example, to climb up and down.

- Climbing is learned by the child on the steps. Begin as simply as possible: let him first try climbing up and down on a pair of low steps or on a low step-ladder or combine a footstool, chair, and table to climb on and off in different stages.
- Increase the difficulty by using a home step-ladder. By the age of 12-14 months, climbing up and down a ladder of 3 feet to 5 feet should be a simple matter.

It is important that the child learn as the first thing to secure himself independently. Observe this patiently, if you can trust him at this. How does he act on higher steps? Does he hold on to the railing? Do not interfere if he might go slowly backwards down the steps. The climbing up of the stairs is automatically connected with the climbing down. The child must understand this. Therefore, climbing activities are important cognitive exercises, that is , they demand intelligence: I can only go up so high from where I can also come down. If the child goes up too high, talk with him, ''How do you think you are going to get down again? Who should help you now?''

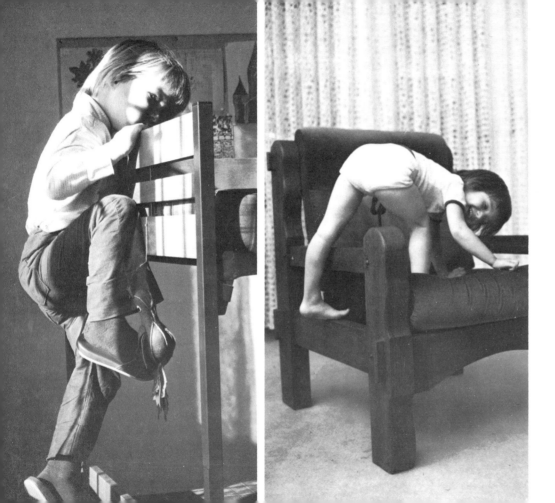

31. Up and Down with Hands and Feet

Our homes are, for the most part, not suited as testing areas for children's play. Several architects have tried to create climbing equipment for small children in the living quarters, which look like elegant pieces of furniture. But as long as we do not yet have the right small equipment, you should put a few pieces of furniture aside for the child's disposal. With hassocks and tables an obstacle course can be built, with pillows and a rug a runway can be laid out. Economical chin up bars fit in every home. Soft elastic pads are more interesting, but also demand more skill. Two- to three-year-olds can, for example, do climbing exercises on an elastic chair. They can:

- climb up from the front or from the side
- climb down head first supported by the hands
- roll off from the seat of the chair to the floor.

Through this, children learn to distribute skillfully their weight and to secure themselves with their hands as well as with their feet. The more opportunities you give your child for safe climbing situations, the sooner you avoid accidents and protect the child from climbing experiences which he cannot master. Children learn through climbing activities to determine their achievement level.

32. Jumping Off (Dismounting)

Jumping begins with children by jumping down from something. They climb up on low walls or curbs and try to jump down. In the home there are also enough possibilities with which to practice jumping (hassock, chair, bed, couch).

Included here is the jump from a bouncy surface which is more difficult, but more tempting. The height from where the child jumps should be about half the child's height. At the beginning you should put down something soft to catch the child, e.g., a soft rug or a mattress.

- The child should practice barefooted.
- Before jumping off he should move about the surface from where he is jumping.
- During the first jumps, you can give him a hand.
- The child learns to jump off without help.
- Climbing up, springing up and down, and jumping off become one smooth, unrestrained movement.
- The child advances to jumping down from other objects or from one place to another, e.g., from a table onto a hassock or onto a couch. By jumping down, the child learns resiliently to catch his body weight and to give in with his joints. Some children use their hands and feet at first when landing; this gives them more certainty since the body weight is distributed more equally in this way and can be better controlled.

33. Crawling Through

Two- and three-year-olds are again and again tempted to crawl through a gate, through a narrow opening, or under an obstacle. Apparently they are attracted by the narrowness or the difficulty involved in trying to make it.

Create similar challenges for the child: let him crawl

- through your straddled legs
- through a vertically held hoop
- between the legs of a chair
- under a bench.

Observe how the child behaves and interfere only if he cannot help himself any further. This should happen seldom. It is better to wait with encouraging words in order to give the child a chance to solve his own problems first.

34. Swinging Back and Forth Independently

Swinging is not only one of the most favorite children's activities, but also an important learning process. The child practices to get himself into the swinging momentum. To do this he has to direct the back and forth motion with his torso. Before you begin to teach swinging, you should show him how he should hold onto the ropes of the swing safely (see also chapter 18). The child must learn that he cannot let his hands loose at will and to hold on so that he can hang his whole body weight on the ropes.

Begin with the swinging in the following way:
- swinging with the help of a push from another
- swinging with one's own momentum
- swinging standing up with the push of the knees
- holding on with only one hand.

Swinging stimulates pleasure. The child feels an accomplishment as he swings higher and higher.

You can buy swings in many different forms. Check them beforehand for their safety factors and all-weather resistance. Children need to learn how to use this apparatus carefully just as others do.

35. Swinging Back and Forth While Hanging from a Bar

Observe how children everywhere exercise on bars. They try strenuously to get on and over them. A horizontal bar has a certain play-stimulating characteristic. The mastered hanging, swinging, up and down swinging strengthen the body muscles and the more sure the child is in the grip and hanging, the more strongly and with greater agility he reacts. Get yourself a horizontal bar. It fits between every door and you can adjust it to the desired height. Children also like to hang and swing on them.

- The more sure the child feels, the more creatively he will react on this apparatus. Instead of hanging by the hands, he may hang by both knees or even one.
- If he should be afraid at first, for example, to let go of the hands in order to hang upside down like a bat, then give him some assistance until he feels more certain.

Do not force the child to do feats at which he himself does not feel secure, but rather encourage him so that he can overcome this barrier independently. Give your child the necessary assurance and strengthen his self-confidence.

Horizontal bars should be offered at different heights, i.e. three feet and four feet. It is ideal when the children can practice on bars between six and nine feet wide on the playground or in the gymnasium. In this way they will not be hindered in climbing over and turning as they are with the narrow bars between the door.

36. Somersaulting and Rolling

Often it begins accidentally: the child bends forward and looks through his legs. He loses his balance and suddenly he rolls forward. The newly discovered fun is repeated, and little by little the child discovers other types of rolling: headover, backwards and sideways, over an obstacle or down a slope.

- Roll with the child in a contest headover or lengthwise like a rolled up rug.
- Roll around in crouched position holding oneself around the shin bones.
- Show him the difference between correct and incorrect rolling: not with a straight, but a rounded back. At first the child often pushes his head into his neck onto the floor instead of tucking in his head and making himself round like a ball.

Through somersaulting and rolling, the child learns agility, flexibility and skillful falling.

37. Sureness of Space Orientation through Ball Playing

The child is stimulated to orient himself to his surroundings through the use of a ball, since he can throw the ball up and down, forward and backward, into the distance, over an obstacle, against a wall, against the floor, through a hoop or through a goal. The ball can be rolled, thrown, kicked, banged, caught. Ball handling also means coordination and reaction ability.

- Choose a ball which fits the size of the child's hand. He must be able to grip it well.

Give the child concrete exercises:

- rolling the ball in a straight line
- rebounding the ball around an obstacle
- throwing the ball at a marked spot on the floor or wall, i.e. into a circle or a triangle
- throwing the ball into a paper basket six to nine feet away.

Use also larger or smaller balls made of different materials for the same exercises.

38. Kickball Games

Kickball games are not only for adults.

It is very typical of the play in which the child uses the ball. A small child can:

- roll the ball with the foot
- kick the ball far away with the foot
- push the ball once with the toes; once with the instep
- alternate with the left and right foot.

Goals for kickball games can be built with pillows or towels toward which the ball can be rolled. Dribble the ball in a contest with the child. If you do not forget to adjust your quickness and ability to that of the child, the child will soon be able to play together with you and with others.

You should think about how much the child needs certain movement abilities in order to play later in a group. Playing is like speaking: you need to be able to make yourself understood.

**SECTION 5: LEARNING
TO USE ONE'S SKILLS**

39. Open Space and Fast Running

Small children need lots of space for running. In small narrow areas they cannot correctly develop their feeling for movement, their space orientation and their speed. The small child must have the chance to run, to race, to run zig-zag, and to react skillfully.

- Let the child run barefooted and, if possible, without clothes.
- Change the surface on which you run with him: run on the grass, on the forest floor, on sand or gravel, on even and uneven surfaces.
- Race with him; play follow me, running away, turning around, weaving.
- Practice sudden changing of direction; run zig-zag. The child gains a steady pace and secure space orientation by running in a spacious area. In running fast, the child keeps his balance with the momentum of his arms and also learns to keep his balance in different running situations. Children who have had sufficient opportunities to run freely, move more self-confidently than those who have been confined to a small space. Most of the children's play areas offer too small a space.

40. Ability to Adjust While Running

The child always needs stimulation to follow moving objects with the eyes, to recognize the speed of the motion, and to adjust his own movement to it. This ability to adjust one's own motion to correspond with that of another can be practiced by a small child with a rolling ball (see also chapter 13), by a two- or three-year-old with a hoop. The child should learn:

- to set a hoop correctly in motion
- to catch up with the hoop again and again
- to independently adjust exactly to the rolling motion of the hoop and to adjust his running speed to that of the hoop: by this he needs to run faster or slower and needs to react correctly to the motion of the hoop.

A two-year-old child can already learn to guide his hoops by himself.

The best way is the following:

- You roll the hoop and follow it together with the child.
- You roll the hoop toward the child.
- The child alone tries to set the hoop into motion.
- The child rolls the hoop along a line which you have marked.
- The child rolls the hoop down a slope.

Change the situation again and again by the use of differently reacting objects. Use also, for example, old wheels from a baby carriage or tricycle, if available.

41. Jumping High

The child practices jumping down at first: he jumps down from somewhere (see chapter 32). He finds jumping up much harder. Here, examples and exercises help which strengthen the imagination of the speed and the jumping off ability.

For example, you make it easier for the child to imagine the high jump if you challenge him to touch something which you hold over him while he jumps up.

- Tie a rope or hold your hand or a toy over the child so that he can try with a high jump to touch it.
- With the first try it is typical that he only stretches his arms above himself while standing still.
- He first has to learn the leap. Show it to him yourself or let other children show him how he can leap with a springy motion out of bended knees. Once having been successful, the effort will be repeated again and again.
- If he has mastered the jump, then you can give him more difficult exercises: jumping forward out of a standing position like a jumping rabbit, from line to line or from tire to tire, jumping on one foot, jumping over an obstacle.

The leaping off with both feet, the so-called standing jump, especially develops the necessary elasticity. Alternate between using both legs, jumping up and down, and hopping on one foot and running jumps in connection with a short and longer approach.

42. Jumping Over Obstacles

After the child has experienced how quickly he must push off the ground and has the feeling for his own body weight through jumping off, he begins to make directed running jumps without hesitation: he jumps

- over an obstacle
- over a ball
- over a steadily held rope
- over a moving rope.

His technique in the running jumps resembles that of an experienced jumper, because he unconsciously carries through the running motion in the jump. Choose resilient floor coverings for jumping.

43. Broad Jumping

The consequent development of the jump in running is the broad jump. It is, however, not so easy for the two- and three-year-old, since he must now get a sense of feeling for the marked jump out of his running motion. The child who has not practiced will simply continue running or stop dead at the point of the leap. Create opportunities for the child to broad jump with a running approach:

- from one stone to another
- from one floor tile to another
- from the rim of the sandbox into the pit
- over a pillow
- over a ditch.

For the leap (jump) the child must make full use of his foot flexibility. He should push off with the whole foot up to the tips of his toes. Unconsciously he balances himself through the counter motion with his arms.

44. Creating New Exercises

Children need time to analyze objects. Observe the ideas the child gets himself and support these with the appropriate stimulation. Many ideas you will first learn through the child; they cannot be found in a pedagogical book. The following are typical exercises on the horizontal bar:

- the attempt to support the feet next to the hands and to swing like a parcel or
- to swing with one foot over the bar to get support
- the attempt to bring the feet backwards between the head and bar and to let go for the dismount to the floor.

If necessary lay a mattress or a foam rubber mat under the bar. However, let the child invent his activities himself. Children who have self-confidence will also be inventive and are likely to have fewer accidents. Do not hold back on praise — but show rebuke or concern if your child becomes too rambunctious.

45. Creativity

In movement activities, the child's fantasy and creativity are shown very impressively. However, he needs ample opportunities repeatedly to set new goals for himself and to experiment with new solutions.

Every teacher knows how inventive children can be on and with certain pieces of equipment. Pedagogical books can be filled with the gymnastic techniques which have been discovered by children on the horizontal bar. How does one get on the horizontal bar without help? How does one get over and around? The same goes for climbing, for games with balls and hoops and also barrels, beams, paper. The layout of an area also invites creativity: how the children use a hill, a ditch, or a sandy place for their games.

The child looks for the activities himself, sometimes motivated by other children, but he solves them without encouragment and urging.

46. Recognition of One's Own Possibilities and Limitations

A part of the child's independence is his ability to recognize his own limitations. He must learn and know: "That I can still do" and "That I cannot." Only in this way, on the one hand, can the child skillfully encounter all problems and, on the other hand, have the courage to discover and look for new things. This experience with his own limitations is made by the child mainly through climbing, since in climbing there is more than just one movement skill. The child experiences how he goes higher and higher with his own strength and always sees the progress made by looking down.

- Give the child many climbing opportunities; above all, with resilient materials: rope ladder, single rope climbing, tree branch.
- Show him also where the dangers are; he must learn not to climb higher than where he can still come down from. Help him to establish his limitations.

Observe your child and intensify the exercises. They should always be in accordance with the child's demands and should not ask for too much. Watch that the child gets the opportunity, the time, and the trust so that he can show you his independence. Every movement exercise should lead to the development of self-confidence.

47. Moving Slowly in a Concentrated Manner

The mastering of slow movements is just as important for the child as the quick, agile reacting. He must be able to measure correctly the tempo of the movement. This activity is difficult for a small child. It demands more concentration and a refined coordination of the discharging of the individual movements. This was also mentioned in walking and running. Give the child the following learning opportunities:

- to carry carefully a cup or can of water
- to go up and down stairs, to step through a hoop, to climb on a chair, or to go around an obstacle with a full cup
- to step carefully over a fragile object
- to carry two full glasses in both hands.

These activities familiarize the child with precision which can be positive for his daily movement behavior. They can also give him as much pleasure and feeling of accomplishment as ball or running games.

48. Types of Sports that Train the Balance

Posture and movement skills are based mainly on the coordination ability. Coordination capabilities are the foundation of equilibrium (balancing). The mastering of balancing plays a special role in the first years of life because the body size and weight as well as the relationship of the growing limbs to the torso change constantly and the child must continually renew his mastering of the equilibrium. Sport types which demand balance are already pursued at the age of three: riding a scooter, ice skating, skiing. Especially interesting for the increasing of balance control are those situations in which the child loses his balance and needs to gain it again. Therefore, observe

- how your child tips off from the scooter and again gets ready for a new start
- how your child falls down when skiing and gets up independently even on an icy slope.

Your child is learning from these situations. Help only in exceptional cases because otherwise you interfere with the child's self-experience.

The goal of our stimulation was to have the child gain self-assuredness and to give him the opportunity to find his way and to skillfully as well as intelligently master a situation. Therefore, he also needs difficulties and defeats in order to learn. An insecure child is usually a child without learning experiences, without practice — have double the patience with him as with a skilled child. Never try to force the child or threaten him in order to accomplish something.

49. Accuracy of Movement

The precise control of a movement is based on its specific flow. Every single part of the movement — dynamics, tempo, direction, flow rhythm — is exactly adjusted to the aim. The exactness of the movement is the result of many attempts. At the beginning, the movements of a small child are mostly measured incorrectly, either over or undercontrolled. Due to the deficiency in precision, there is not only a lack of coordination but sometimes also a lack of muscle strength, mobility, or other prerequisites.

Through different exercises, the child can practice his movement accuracy. At the same time, the adults can check how skillful the child is:

- to step between two ropes without touching them
- to guide a balloon within the room to a designated spot
- to go along a narrow rim without stumbling
- to jump like a jumping jack, that is, spreading legs apart and simultaneously clapping the hands above the head and then bringing both hands and legs together again
- to touch the forehead against the raised knee in a standing position
- not to bump against objects in a dark room.

It is important for the child in the learning of movement accuracy to master precisely different movement processes. They should not exercise monotonously.

50. The Child Needs To Learn in a Group

Learning is *always* a social process: the child learns from others and with others. He learns through observing, comparing and imitating. Comparing oneself to others becomes more and more the standard for one's own performance. The competition with others also belongs to daily life situations. The child must be matched up to this. He learns to strive toward good performances; however, he also knows that others can perform better in some areas. The orientation to his peer group, to older and younger children is equally important for the child.

It is typical for small children to squat together in a group while playing. The necessary order results through the fact that they arrange themselves leisurely, never "rank and file." Children should, therefore, not be forced into forms of order which are not appropriate. They must, however, learn to observe certain regulations of common interest to the group and to create rules for their games, i.e.:

- to obey given rules
- to take turns on an apparatus
- not to hinder the other
- to put away toys and equipment which they have played with and on
- not to destroy things which are also important for other children.

The child learns the rules of society only through the group. Let your child, therefore, gather experience with other children, positive as well as negative. The goal of this training is the independence of the child. When your child says to you, "Leave me alone, I can do it by myself," then you have gone another big step further.

Pictorial References:

Cover photo and Numbers 1 and 10, left and right: Publications Studio, Washington, D.C.

Numbers 3, 5 left, 7 above, 8, 14, 17, 24, 26, 29, 39: Christa Pilger-Feiler, Munich; Numbers 4, 7 below, 13, 28 left, 30 right: Nestle; Numbers 18, 19, 21, 23 left, 25, 27, 28 right, 31 left, 34, 35, 37 right, 38, 40, 41, 42, 43, 45, 59: Gerhard Schmidt, Vienna; all remaining photos: Archives of the German Sportscollege, Cologne, West Germany (of those Number 5 right, 6, 9, 11, 20, 22, 23 right, 32, 37 left by Klaus Bala; Numbers 15, 46, 50 by Mitsuda).

ALSO AVAILABLE FROM AAHPER:

ANNOTATED BIBLIOGRAPHY ON MOVEMENT EDUCATION

A collection of selected resources significant to a deeper understanding of the many aspects and definitions of movement education. Designed to serve a variety of professional needs — for a beginning specialist, experienced practitioner, classroom teacher or any student of human movement. Listings are organized under major classifications of Theory and Practice. The latter is sub-divided to cover basic movement, dance-drama, gymnastics, and sport.

CHILDREN LEARN PHYSICAL SKILLS

Learning programs designed to provide parents, teachers, and specialists with techniques and suggestions for developing movement abilities in early childhood. Two separate volumes are available — one for use with infants, from birth to 3 years, and the other for children, ages 3-5 years. The activities, organized in systematically planned "sessions," are directed toward open learning situations in which children can gain self-confidence through movement. By Liselott Diem, internationally recognized authority in the field (translated from the original volumes in German).

FOUNDATIONS AND PRACTICES IN PERCEPTUAL-MOTOR LEARNING: A QUEST FOR UNDERSTANDING

A multi-disciplinary examination of major conceptual viewpoints of perceptual-motor behavior and teaching methods. Includes descriptions of action programs, tests, resource materials and a professional preparation survey.

MOVEMENT ACTIVITIES FOR PLACES AND SPACES

A new book for the physical education specialist, classroom teacher, and professional preparation department. Offers methods and activities in physical education which can contribute to each child's maximum development. Designed to encourage development of motor skills, create situations in which children can make choices in an atmosphere of freedom, and allow children to participate in enjoyable movement experiences which help to develop a desire for continued participation in physical activities.

ECHOES OF INFLUENCE FOR ELEMENTARY SCHOOL PHYSICAL EDUCATION

A publication which brings together some of the best that has been written and said about physical education in the elementary school since 1970. Includes selected papers and articles identifying and exploring contemporary issues, research findings, and differing points of view about many topics — from both practical and philosophical points of view. An excellent resource for anyone interested in physical education for children.

For Price and Order Information, write:
AAHPER
1201 16th St., N.W.
Washington, D.C. 20036

WHO CAN . . .

Twenty series of pictures, with text, illustrating education for movement in the primary grades. Offers a selection of basic activity forms — with variations and progression — which are based on movements fundamental to more complicated patterns as evidenced in more refined specific sports skills. The activities presented embody creative approaches to the traditional, meeting the needs of children to discover how to use their bodies efficiently. The activities covered require only simple equipment that can be used in and out of the gymnasium. Designed for use by the classroom teacher, advanced or beginning specialist, and in courses of professional preparation. By Liselott Diem, internationally recognized authority in the field.

ANNOTATED BIBLIOGRAPHY ON PERCEPTUAL-MOTOR DEVELOPMENT

An up-to-date bibliography with sections devoted to auditory perception and movement; body image and movement; and depth-distance perception and movement. A separate compilation of tests, programs, material sources, assessment instruments and films is included.

YOUTH SPORTS GUIDE — FOR COACHES AND PARENTS

Intended for parents, volunteer coaches and youth sports administrators, this is the first comprehensive coaching manual to be produced by a national association for the youth sports field (both boys and girls) in the United States. It covers such topics as development of fundamental skills, physical and physiological development, psychological considerations, instructional strategies, preparation for competition, motivation, managing a team, and the issues of winning and losing. The content is easily understood and appropriate for any of the youth sports, including softball, baseball, basketball, football, soccer, hockey, swimming, tennis, and bowling. Edited by Jerry Thomas of Louisiana State University with contributions from some of the top sports educators, researchers, and child development experts in the country. Produced in cooperation with The Manufacturers Life Insurance Company (ManuLife) of Canada.

CHILDREN'S DANCE

What happens when children dance? They feel good about each other and themselves. They gain a sense of creativity, responsiveness communication. CHILDREN'S DANCE, an AAHPER publication, reflects the joys of children dancing. It's about ways teachers can use dance in their classrooms in lively, innovative ways. How can dance help increase ethnic understanding? What is its relationship to other arts and science? Do you think boys can't dance? What dance experiences should be providing? How would you portray, through dance, a bowl of spaghetti . . . a chess game . . . a creature called a "damp, despised, and aimless Doze?"

TWO NEW GUIDES FOR HELPING VISUALLY HANDICAPPED CHILDREN GROW:

GET A WIGGLE ON

A new booklet prepared to assist teachers, parents, and others who are in contact with blind or visually impaired infants. It contains suggestions which will be helpful in assisting these children, early in their lives, to grow and learn like other children. The suggestions are presented in the form of requests from the baby. For example: "Pick me up and carry me about. Unless you do, I will probably lie very quietly in my crib. I will be listening, but I won't know what the sounds are or if they have meaning. Soon I may stop paying attention to what I hear. I need you — to give meaning to my world."

MOVE IT!!!

Prepared as a sequel to the above publication, with additional suggestions for assisting blind or visually handicapped children who have "gotten a wiggle on" and are ready to "move it!" One of the child's many suggestions: "I want to be strong. Help me to develop my strength. Give me things to carry, push, and pull. Shovels to dig with, balls to throw. Let me climb up jungle gyms and hang from the trapeze. Let me push the merry-go-round, push someone on the swing, pull the wagon. Let me hang by my hands from a limb. Give me a chance to use all my muscles. I gotta learn to carry my own weight — and use it."